Un common Animals

ARCTIC FOX

Very Cool!

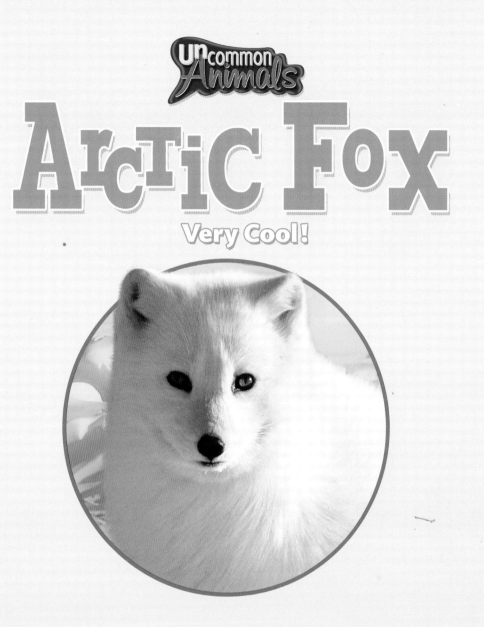

by Stephen Person

Consultant: Dr. Maarten J. J. E. Loonen

BEARPORT PUBLISHING

New York, New York

Credits

Cover and Title Page, © Altrendo Nature/Getty Images; TOC, © Mark Newman/SuperStock; 4, © Clark James Mishler/AlaskaStock.com; 5, © J.Mallwitz/WILDLIFE/Peter Arnold Inc.; 6, © www.arcticstation.nl/Ronald J.W. Visser; 8, www.arcticstation.nl/Maarten J.J.E. Loonen; 9, © www.arcticstation.nl/Maarten J.J.E. Loonen; 10, © Claude Steelman/Oxford Scientific/Photolibrary; 11, © Lynn Stone/Animals Animals-Earth Scenes; 12, © Paul Nicklen/National Geographic/Getty Images; 13T, © Chris Hendrickson/Masterfile; 13B, © Klein/Hubert/Peter Arnold Inc.; 14, © Gary Shultz/AlaskaStock.com; 15T, © Nicolas Lecomte; 15B, ©Robert H. Armstrong/Animals Animals-Earth Scenes; 16, © Jeff Shultz/AlaskaStock.com; 17, © Norbert Rosing/National Geographic/Getty Images; 18, © Johnny Johnson/AlaskaStock.com; 19, © Norbert Rosing/Animals Animals-Earth Scenes; 20, © Alan & Sandy Carey/zefa/Corbis; 21, © Owen Newman/Oxford Scientific/Photolibrary; 22, © Kenneth R. Whitten/AlaskaStock.com; 23, © John Conrad/Corbis; 24, © Steven Kazlowski/AlaskaStock.com; 25, © Dan Guravich/Photo Researchers, Inc.; 26, © Michio Hoshino/Minden Pictures; 27, © Nicholas J. Fucci/AlaskaStock.com; 28, © Yva Momatiuk & John Eastcott/Minden Pictures; 29T, © Nigel Bean/npl/Minden Pictures; 29B, © Michio Hoshino/Minden Pictures; 31, © Sam Chadwick/Shutterstock; 32 © John Pitcher/iStockphoto.

Publisher: Kenn Goin
Senior Editor: Lisa Wiseman
Creative Director: Spencer Brinker
Original Design: Dawn Beard Creative
Photo Researcher: Amy Dunleavy

Library of Congress Cataloging-in-Publication Data

Person, Stephen.
  Arctic fox : very cool! / by Stephen Person.
      p. cm. — (Uncommon animals)
  Includes bibliographical references and index.
  ISBN-13: 978-1-59716-730-7 (library binding)
  ISBN-10: 1-59716-730-4 (library binding)
  1. Arctic fox—Juvenile literature. I. Title.

  QL737.C22P448 2009
  599.776'4—dc22

                    2008010637

For more information, write to Bearport Publishing Company, Inc., 101 Fifth Avenue, Suite 6R, New York, New York, 10003. Printed in the United States of America.

10 9 8 7 6 5 4 3 2

Contents

The Chase Is On!

In the Arctic, **biologist** Maarten Loonen watched as a group of geese led their young toward a lake. Maarten looked around. He had a feeling that he wasn't the only one watching these birds. Suddenly he saw a flash of gray. It was an Arctic fox!

The Arctic fox's speed helps it catch birds and other small animals.

The fox darted into the group of birds, snapping its jaws. Too young to fly away, the **goslings** scattered and swerved to avoid the attacker. "The rest of the flock sprinted toward the nearest water at top speed," said Maarten. Running as fast as he could, Maarten followed the chase.

Arctic geese

Arctic geese and other birds are an important source of food for Arctic foxes.

Living with Foxes

Maarten watched as the Arctic fox caught a few of the goslings. Then he saw the fox dig a hole and bury the dead birds. Hidden food supplies, such as these, are called **caches**. This fox will need many caches to survive the long cold Arctic winter, when there is little food available.

Maarten Loonen lives in the Arctic during the summer.

Maarten has been studying Arctic wildlife since 1990. Every summer, he travels from his home in the Netherlands to the **Arctic region**. There, he lives in Ny-Ålesund, Norway—the northernmost town in the world. This is a great place to study Arctic animals. "In my town, there is a pair of foxes under my neighbor's house," Maarten says. "I see the young foxes every day in July and August."

Arctic Foxes in the Wild

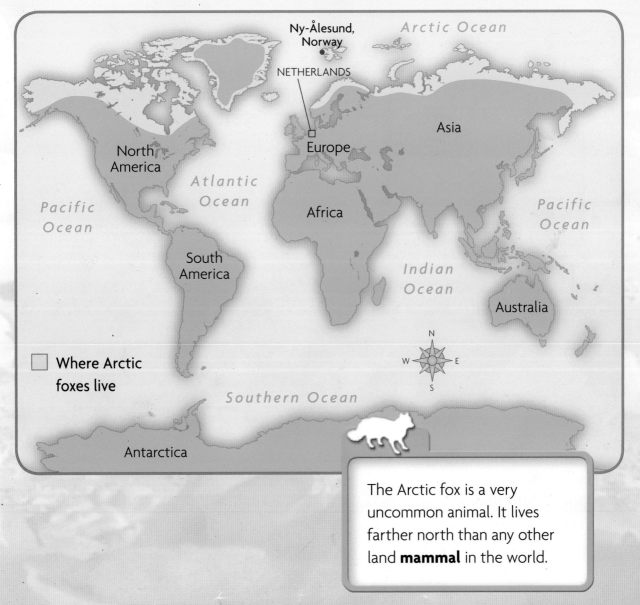

Ny-Ålesund, Norway

Arctic Ocean

NETHERLANDS

Europe

Asia

North America

Atlantic Ocean

Africa

Pacific Ocean

Pacific Ocean

South America

Indian Ocean

Australia

☐ Where Arctic foxes live

Southern Ocean

N
W   E
S

Antarctica

The Arctic fox is a very uncommon animal. It lives farther north than any other land **mammal** in the world.

A Lot to Learn

Maarten has learned a lot about Arctic foxes by studying the same ones year after year. Each July, he and a group of **researchers** carefully trap the foxes. Every fox is weighed and given a name. A color tag is placed in each ear. The tags help Maarten keep track of the foxes from year to year. He can learn where each animal has traveled and how much he or she has grown.

Maarten tagging a young fox

Maarten is always discovering how smart and tough these foxes are. They have to be. In the Arctic, winter lasts for eight months. Powerful snowstorms are common and temperatures can fall to −58°F (−50°C). How can any animal survive in a **climate** like this?

During much of the Arctic winter, the sun doesn't rise. It's dark 24 hours a day! In the area where Maarten does his research, there are about 18 weeks each summer when the sun doesn't set at all!

Maarten letting a fox go after tagging it

Built for the Cold

The Arctic fox survives in the **extreme** cold because it has the warmest fur of any mammal in the world. Even the tips of its paws are covered in fur. The fur keeps the fox so warm that it usually sleeps right out in the open, using its long bushy tail as a blanket.

The fox uses its long furry tail to help keep warm in the winter.

Sometimes the weather does get too cold, even for an Arctic fox. When this happens, the animal digs a hole in the snow to escape the freezing wind. A fox doesn't need to do this often, though. "The Arctic fox is well **adapted** to the harsh winter," Maarten says.

The Arctic fox's nose and ears are short. Having ears and a nose close to its body helps keep heat from escaping.

A Fox of Many Colors

Maarten is not as well adapted to the harsh winter as the Arctic fox. When temperatures start falling in September, he heads back home to the Netherlands. How does the Arctic fox prepare for the cold weather? It changes its fur.

During the summer, a fox's coat is brown and gray and thin. In September, the fox's coat starts to grow thicker. Its color also changes. By November, the animal has very fluffy white fur to keep it warm. Then at the end of winter, the fox **sheds** its fur and grows a darker, thinner summer coat.

An Arctic fox with its thick winter coat

The fox's different coats come in handy when it's hunting. The winter fur blends in with the white snow. The brown and gray coat can't be seen against the rocks and dirt of summer. This **camouflage** allows the fox to sneak up on its **prey** all year-round.

An Arctic fox's coat between winter and summer

An Arctic fox with its thinner summer coat

By eating a lot at the end of summer, a fox can add several pounds of body fat. This fat, along with its fur, acts as **insulation**, keeping the fox's body warm during winter.

Not Picky Eaters

The fox's fur may help it hunt, but it's still difficult for the animal to find prey. There's not much food in the Arctic. Foxes have to eat anything they can find, including berries, seaweed, and insects.

Arctic foxes use their strong sense of hearing and smell to find prey beneath the snow.

During his research, Maarten discovered that the fox is an expert **predator**. With one quick pounce, it snatches birds, fish, and **lemmings**. Foxes will even steal birds' eggs and hide them in caches. When there is no food nearby, they have to go looking for it. Biologists watched one fox travel as far as 1,400 miles (2,253 km) in search of food.

This fox heads to its cache with a goose egg.

A lemming

Arctic foxes are also **scavengers**. They eat dead reindeer, seals, and other large animals.

Family Time

Maarten has seen Arctic foxes work extra hard to find food when they're raising their young. Adult male and female foxes get ready to start families in March or April. They work together to clean out a **den**.

An Arctic fox den

Many dens have been used by different fox families for 300 years or more. Some large dens have as many as 100 entrances.

Fox **cubs** are born in May or June. The parents have a **litter** of 7 to 15 cubs. Both parents take turns hunting for small animals, such as lemmings, to feed to their young. The parents have to catch as many as 100 lemmings a day to keep themselves and their hungry cubs alive.

An Arctic fox returns from a successful hunt.

A Very Short Childhood

Adult foxes know that their young are helpless. Cubs are born blind, and they depend on their parents for food. They are easy prey for predators, such as golden eagles. After the cubs are born, "the parents are usually very secretive, and hide with the cubs in the den," explains Maarten.

Young foxes at the entrance of their den

When they're one month old, young foxes begin poking their heads out of the den. If they hear a parent bark suddenly, they know to jump back inside. The bark may be a warning that an eagle is nearby.

After two months of having food brought to them by their parents, young foxes begin hunting. They have to learn quickly. When winter comes, they will move out of the den and have to survive on their own.

Young foxes learning to hunt through play

Arctic fox parents stay together throughout their adult lives. They often use the same den year after year.

A World of Danger

Winter is a very dangerous time for young and old Arctic foxes. "For foxes, winter survival is so difficult," Maarten says. Not only do they have to face the cold but they have to watch out for predators such as wolves or polar bears.

An Arctic wolf

Foxes have to beware of people, too. "There is a lot of fur trapping in winter," says Maarten. Trappers catch foxes for their thick white fur, which is used to make hats, mittens, and coats. Despite all the dangers, the **population** of this Arctic animal is not falling. As long as there is enough food, the number of foxes should stay strong.

Foxes are trapped in winter, when their fur is thickest.

Arctic foxes' large litters also help keep their population from falling.

No Heat, Please!

Although the population is **stable** now, another danger looms ahead for the Arctic fox. The climate is changing and Earth is slowly getting warmer. Scientists think temperatures will keep rising in the Arctic and around the world. This could be bad news for the Arctic fox.

The Arctic fox is perfectly adapted to life on the snow and ice.

Higher temperatures in the Arctic are also a danger to polar bears. Bears live and hunt on sea ice. Climate change is causing this ice to slowly melt.

If the Arctic gets just a few degrees warmer, red foxes may start moving north. Red foxes usually live in warmer **habitats**, but they could survive in the Arctic if temperatures rise there. These animals are twice as big as Arctic foxes. They could take over the foxes' dens and hunting areas, leaving them hungry and homeless. Red foxes may even attack and kill Arctic foxes.

Red foxes are used to living in warmer habitats.

The Hardest Time of All

Climate change may eventually be the biggest threat to the Arctic fox. For now, though, "the end of winter is the most difficult time," says Maarten. A fox's food cache is often empty by this point. Sometimes a fox has only one way to find food—snatching it from a polar bear.

A hungry fox takes a huge risk following a polar bear for a free meal.

A hungry fox will creep up close to a huge polar bear. It waits and watches as the bear hunts for seals. Sometimes the bear will kill a seal and leave some meat behind. At other times, the fox will steal a bit of the bear's food as it eats. The fox will try to run away if the bear notices. If the fox is unlucky, it could become the bear's next meal.

Foxes are usually quicker tha[n] bears during short runs.

Just how hard is it to survive in the Arctic? Arctic foxes live only about three years in the wild. In the safety of zoos, these same animals live for ten years or more.

Outfoxing the Arctic

When the warmer weather returns, Maarten moves back to the Arctic to continue his studies. He's always excited to see the new families of foxes. "They are not afraid of people," he says. "We see the cubs daily. They're beautiful and playful."

These cubs will soon face their first winter.

The young cubs may be having fun now. Another winter is on the way, however. The cubs have only a few months to learn how to live in one of the **harshest** habitats on Earth. What does Maarten think is the most amazing fact about the Arctic fox? That's easy: "It can survive the Arctic winter," he says.

The Arctic fox is a member of the canid family, which includes foxes, wolves, and dogs.

Arctic Fox Facts

The Arctic fox lives farther north than any other land mammal. It can survive temperatures as low as −58°F (−50°C). Arctic foxes are able to live in these harsh conditions because they have the warmest fur of any animal. Here are some other facts about this uncommon animal.

Weight	6–17 pounds (3–8 kg)
Length	**head and body:** 18–27 inches (46–69 cm) **tail:** 14 inches (36 cm)
Fur Color	**winter coat:** white **summer coat:** brown and gray
Food	lemmings, birds' eggs, birds, fish, insects, dead animals, berries, seaweed, and scraps from polar bear kills such as seals
Life Span	about 3 years in the wild; 10 years or more in zoos
Habitat	Arctic region
Population	about 300,000

More Uncommon Animals

The Arctic fox is one kind of uncommon animal in the Arctic region. Many other unusual animals also live there.

Reindeer

- Reindeer, also called caribou, live in herds as large as 500,000.
- They are about 4 feet (1.2 m) at the shoulder and weigh as much as 550 pounds (249 kg).
- Both males and females have antlers, which can grow up to 5 feet (1.5 m) long. They use their antlers to fight other reindeer, and to defend their territory or food.
- In some areas of northern Europe, reindeer have been tamed. People use them to carry heavy loads. They also use them for their meat and milk.

Polar Bear

- Polar bears grow to be about 5 feet (1.5 m) tall at the shoulder and weigh 900 to 1,600 pounds (408 to 726 kg).
- They eat only meat. They dig out baby seals resting under the snow or attack swimming seals or whales that come to the water's surface for air.
- To help them stay warm, polar bears have black skin, which absorbs heat from the sun. They also have a thick layer of fat under their skin.
- Polar bears have no natural predators. They don't fear humans and have been known to kill people.

Glossary

adapted (uh-DAP-tid) changed because of the environment or conditions; changed over time to be fit for the environment

Arctic region (ARK-tic REE-juhn) the northernmost area on Earth; it includes the Arctic Ocean, the North Pole, and northern parts of Europe, Asia, and North America; one of the coldest areas in the world

biologist (bye-OL-uh-jist) a scientist who studies plants or animals

caches (KASH-iz) hidden supplies of food that are stored for later use

camouflage (KAM-uh-flazh) the fur or skin that makes animals or people look like and blend into their surroundings

climate (KLYE-mit) the typical weather in a place

cubs (KUHBZ) baby foxes

den (DEN) an animal's home; a hidden place where an animal sleeps or has its babies

extreme (ek-STREEM) very great or severe

goslings (GAHS-lingz) young geese

habitats (HAB-uh-*tats*) places in nature where a plant or animal normally lives

harshest (HAHR-shist) the most severe or uncomfortable

insulation (*in*-suh-LAY-shun) something that prevents heat from escaping

lemmings (LEM-ingz) tiny animals, similar to mice, that live in the far northern regions of the world

litter (LIT-ur) a group of foxes born at the same time to the same mother

mammal (MAM-uhl) a warm-blooded animal that has a backbone, hair or fur on its skin, and drinks its mother's milk as a baby

population (*pop*-yuh-LAY-shuhn) the total number of a kind of animal living in a place

predator (PRED-uh-tur) an animal that hunts other animals for food

prey (PRAY) animals that are hunted or caught for food

researchers (REE-sur-churz) people who study things or collect information

scavengers (SKAV-uhn-jurz) animals that feed on the dead bodies of other animals

sheds (SHEDZ) loses something, such as fur

stable (STAY-buhl) firm and steady

Bibliography

Glick, Daniel. "Global Warming S.O.S." *Audubon Magazine* (November–December 2007).

www.arcticstation.nl

Read More

Alexander, Bryan and Cherry. *Journey into the Arctic.* New York: Oxford University Press (2003).

Darling, Kathy. *Arctic Babies.* New York: Walker & Company (1997).

Guigon, Catherine. *The Arctic.* New York: Abrams Books for Young Readers (2007).

Townsend, Emily Rose. *Arctic Foxes.* Mankato, MN: Capstone Press (2006).

Learn More Online

To learn more about Arctic foxes, visit
www.bearportpublishing.com/UncommonAnimals

Index

About the Author

Stephen Person has written many textbooks, as well as children's books about American history. He lives in Brooklyn with his wife, Rachel, and their daughter, Anna.